Ana Tereza Želinski

The First World War in the context of bećarac

Ana Tereza Želinski

The First World War in the context of bećarac

A true story through verses

JustFiction Edition

Imprint

Any brand names and product names mentioned in this book are subject to trademark, brand or patent protection and are trademarks or registered trademarks of their respective holders. The use of brand names, product names, common names, trade names, product descriptions etc. even without a particular marking in this work is in no way to be construed to mean that such names may be regarded as unrestricted in respect of trademark and brand protection legislation and could thus be used by anyone.

Cover image: www.ingimage.com

Publisher:
JustFiction! Edition
is a trademark of
International Book Market Service Ltd., member of OmniScriptum Publishing Group
17 Meldrum Street, Beau Bassin 71504, Mauritius
Printed at: see last page
ISBN: 978-620-0-49351-4

,,I saw the light fade from the sky
On the wind I heard a sigh
As the snowflakes cover my fallen brothers
I will say this last goodbye

Night is now falling
So ends this day
The road is now calling
And I must away
Over hill and under tree
Through lands where never light has shone
By silver streams that run down to the sea

Under cloud, beneath the stars
Over snow one winter's morn
I turn at last to paths that lead home ...

Billy Boyd

To All Who Have Lost A Loved One.

Contents

Introduction

Bećarac is a minimal traditional vocal-instrumental song or a sung record. It consists of two rhymed decasyllables. This song structure is characteristic of the eastern part of the Republic of Croatia, more precisely Slavonia, Baranya and Syrmia. *Bećarac* is a part of each situation[1] in the world of *Šokci*. It entertaints the recipient and informs them, e.g. it implicitly tells them about an attitude towards something, the worldview or the facts, and it provokes information, reaction, or attitude towards someone or something. Since the content of *bećarac* contains elements of documented reality and pieces of information, because its text is built around events which are more or less current, we may say that it is an authentic artefact of historical events.

Picture 1. Emperor Karlo and empress Zita

---

[1] During proposals, weddings, village parties, church celebrations, road patrols, traditional gatherings such as *pudarenje* and *divani*, various jobs such as separating goose feathers (*čijalo),* ploughing, reaping, harvesting, digging, keeping the cattle out to pasture, as well as in time of Christmas and Easter.

Care Karlo i carice Zita,[2]

šta ratuješ, kad nemate žita.

(Emperor Karl and empress Zita,

Why are you in a battle, when there's no wheat?)[3]

Janje moje ranjeno kraj Drine,

ranito je iz gevermašine.

(My lamb was shot near Drina,

it was shot from the machine gun)

Picture 2. Scenes from the First World War

---

[2] The author thought that it would be important to give explanations of some distichs, which does not imply that readers or interpreters will have the same interpretation.

[3] The verses are translated literally (bećarac is written in decasyllabic verses which ryhme) [transl. note].

Sinoć meni dojde karta mala,

da su moga ranili bećara.

(Last night I received a card,

Saying that my man was wounded.)

Bećarac reveals data on the emotional state of the speaker, time and place of the event, and the information on history, politics, economy and current social issues. It is explicitly defined by the fact that it is recited by *someone* who has been through a certain life and social experience. Therefore it has been the object of this paper's analysis.

Approach to the text and methodology

This paper analyses the texts with historical themes from the beginning of the 20th century by Luka Lukić and Slavko Janković. Through interpretative and comparative methods it will analyse the war discourse of the historical events during the World War I, particularly the direct and indirect war participants, places of battle, imprisonments, war methods, weapons of war, and political and economic situation. Besides that, the texts reveal emotional and physical states of women, and through women figures differences in working class are observed.[4]

Very often women show the fear and uncertainty of this world disaster, the collective catastrophe which happened on almost every continent, and started with the assassination of Austro-Hungarian crown prince, archduke Franz Ferdinand and his wife Sofia Chotek, duchess of Hohenberg, on June 28, 1914.

---

[4] More about the changes in the working class structure, the emancipation, and women rights in Hutinec, G., *Prvi svjetski rat i poslijeratna Europa* (1914. – 1936.), book 16, 126.

Picture 3. The assassination of Austro-Hungarian crown prince, archduke Franz Ferdinand and his wife Sofia Chotek

How did the local (civil) population see the First World War?

The view of local (civil) population should be divided into two stages. First, there was a general enthusiastic acceptance of war motivated by fierce battles which served as a way to express dissatisfaction with the border enemies[5] or ruling elites.

Immediately after the beginning of the war, all governments, all Secretaries of State, without exception, have urged people to the sacred unity, heroism, and love towards their country, and encouraged hatred towards the enemy. [...] ˙Politics of all war-affected countries focused on creating the atmosphere of political, social and religious unity, solidarity and necessity of making the greatest sacrifice if necessary... (Kardum 2009:88-89).

---

[5] By the secret London agreement in April 1915, the Allied Powers promised Italy big parts of the east Adriatic coast, all the way to cape Ploče south of Šibenik and numerous Croatian islands and Croatian hinterland territories in return for leaving Central Powers and joining them. More in Goldstein, I., *Hrvatska povijest*, Book 21, 317.

Da je dati s dikom vojevati,
ja bi mala s mojim vojevala.[6]

(If I could be in the battle next to my darling,
I would, although I am small)

Pitaje me, koje j' dika vojske?
Domobranac dvadesetiosme.

(They ask me what army my darling is in,
he is in the Home Guard 28th Regiment)

Koji nose crvene parole,
to su same bekrije i lole.[7]

(Who carries red slogans,
all cheerful Slavonian men)

---

[6] Women were prohibited from warfare, but they would join gladly, carried by the initial enthusiasm.
[7] In the Austro-Hungarian army regiments had colourful *slogans*, i.e. a foursquare piece of cloth in the necklace. The verse speaks of debauchery and flashiness of soldiers.

Picture 4. The 28th Home Guard Osijek Infantry Regiment

According to the Monarchy mobilisation plans, people of Brod belonged (as a part of the common army) to the mobilisation centre of the 78th Infantry Regiment seated in Osijek, whereas the Home Guard members were in the 28th Home Guard Infantry Regiment, which was also seated in Osijek (catalogue *Dadoh zlato za željezo* 2011: 25-30).

Šinje ječe, ajziban se kreće,
ode moje u soldate cveće.

(Rail track sound is loud, train is moving,
my darling is going to the army)

Šinje zveče, ajziban se čuje,
moje lane u vojsku putuje.

(Rail track sound is loud, you can hear the train,

my darling is going to the army)

Eroplane, ne leti po zraku,

ostat će mi dika u oblaku.[8]

(Aeroplane, don't fly,

my darling will stay in the sky)

Curo moja, ti ne roni suza,

lipo stoji domobranska bluza.[9]

(Hey girl, don't cry,

the Home Guard shirt looks nice)

Picture 5. Farewell from the soldiers

---

[8] These lines talk about the initial enthusiasm (head in the clouds) and joy of going to the army to defend their country.

[9] The soldier belongs the the 28th Home Guard Infantry Regiment with Croatian command, seated in Osijek.

The second phase encompasses general numbness, fatigue and war anxiety. The hope of a quick resolution of war turmoil disappeared after launching and building of war industry and constant new mobilisations, because the existing armies that had been prepared for Blitzkrieg were not sufficient. This only deepened the general and continuing suffering, economic collapse, and social disaster, because the new recruitments led to the lack of the labour force in the country, and there were vast agricultural areas that were left untreated.

The long war was not expected and therefore the mobilisation stopped economic life completely [...] Industrial and agricultural labour force poured towards the battlefields by trains, the production and trade was stopped [...] Military needs got bigger every day and they needed to be coordinated to the needs of civilians (Kardum 2009: 109).

Care Karlo i carice Zita,
šta ratuješ, kad nemate žita.

(Emperor Karlo and empress Zita,
Why are you in a battle, when there's no wheat?)

Kapetane, pusti moje janje,
za jednoga ni više ni manje.

(Captain, let my lamb go,
one more or less.)

The consequences of the First World War on the lifestyle of local (civil) population

Picture 6. Poverty of the population[10]

The consequences of this general, continuing destruction are innumerable; a large number of fallen soldiers[11], the disabled, the mentally ill, those suffering from

---

[10] Image translation: *Oh, great God, this will be enough for me for a whole week.*

[11] MacMillan (2008) talks about some 1,290,000 Austro-Hungarian soldiers. Krile (2014) says that there is a "rough estimation of 137 thousands of Croatian soldiers who were killed in different battlefields from 1914 to 1918, and around 109 thousand of Croatian civilians who died due to war actions, epidemics, or hunger."

typhoid fever, cholera and influenza[12], and almost every other woman wearing mourning clothes. There was a shortage of raw materials, grain[13], food, and other basic necessities for the sheer survival.

The war has left behind closed factories, fallow fields, destroyed bridges and railways. There were shortages of fertilizers, seeds, and raw materials. [...] In all parts of Europe officials and private relief agencies sent disturbing reports about the millions of unemployed, the desperate housewives feeding their families potatoes and cabbage soup, the starving children. [...] All across the former Austro-Hungary hospitals ran out of bandages and medicine. [...] People would eat coal dust, sawdust, sand (MacMillan 2008: 93).

Dugi dani, a komisi[14] mali,
al' je teško, kog država 'rani.[15]

(Long days and small pieces of bread,
it's difficult to those who are fed by the government)

There was a general decrease in the quality of life and work, and the difficult country life got even more difficult.[16] Up to that time, women had had the role of wives and mothers, but due to the great number of recruited men they became central persons in the family, taking care of the senoirs and the young ones. Their inferior role was put to an end, and they took on greater responsibilities through the reverse of

---

[12] These events and meetings with numerous sick people were described by Ivana Brlić Mažuranić in her letters, in which she describes "terrible appearance" of a transport of soldiers suffering from typhoid who came to Brod for treatment. More in Preslika arhiva obitelji Brlić, box 74, cluster 7, recording DD00103101.

[13] Janković (1967) says „Austro-Hungarian government has brough regulations on requisitioning of grain, especially wheat. Under these regulations, one had to make an inventory of all grain immediately after the harvest. The minimum was left to the peasant, according to the seeding needs and the number of household members. Everything else had to be handed over to the authorities at low price".

[14] Military bread.

[15] Difficult situation in the agriculture and economy; general crisis in the state.

[16] More in Lukić, L. *Crtice ili zapiske iz rata 1915.-1918.,* E7T/19, 33, MBP.

the family roles.[17] Therefore, in the times of the most awful battles, it was not unusal to see women perform jobs that had been strictly male up to then. As the city and country rumours talked about the corrupt behaviour of the governing, some women took advantage of that.

U mene su sa zlatom papuče,
moja dika na molbu kod kuće.[18]

(I have slippers with golden threads,
my baby will be back home if I ask)

Imala sam nešto malo zlata,
pa sam dala caru za soldata.

(I had some gold and
I gave it to the emperor for my soldier)

Ja ću pisat sedmorice stolu,
da mi diku ljubiti dozvolu.[19]

(I will write to the Table of Seven,
to give me permission to kiss my darling)

The agriculture was an important part of the economy then, and apart from the lack of workforce, bad weather also contributed to the difficult situation in

---

[17] More in Hutinec, G., *Prvi svjetski rat i poslijeratna Europa* (1914.-1936.), Book 16, 126.
[18] Women bribed the superiors with gold to let their parners home. These men were called 'reklamants'.
[19] In Austria-Hungary the Supreme Court was called Stol sedmorice, i.e. The Table of Seven.

agriculture. Crop yield was low, barely sufficient for survival (Cafuta 2014: 6). (…) Year 1914 was horrible due to World War I, and very sad in itself (…) To put it shortly, misery and disaster all around. (…) Spring (1915) was rainy, and it was difficult to seed; more difficult with people on the battle field, all the healthy and strong were on the battle field and in the army, and old people, children and women were at home and there was no workforce which could do the strenuous jobs. (Biber 2003: 277).

U ratu su momci i vojnici,
svi dilberi, mladi zipcigeri.[20]

(Young guys and soldiers are in the war,
all handsome, young zipciger soldiers)

There is a slight lack of discipline, and people find even the smallest ways to exit. There is no bread. It should be produced in greater quantities. Richer people (according to a regulation) are let go from the army to increase the yield (the older ones of course). They are so called *reklamants*. This is an opportunity for notaries to earn a lot. Armies that had been created for decades start falling apart, doctors help people get out, corruption becomes established, smuggling starts to flourish, millions are made because country does not have time to ask for the price, but simply prints money (Janković 1970: 136).

Sad se stare pobijaju banke,
moga diku ljube Talijanke.[21]

---

[20] There were no young men in the villages then; zipciger is the name of soldiers of the 70th Regiment of the joint army in Austro-Hungary.
[21] There was an inflation caused by the change of paper money. At that time Austrian army penetrated deep into Italy.

(The old banks fight,

my darling is kissed by Italian women)

Because of war the price of cattle, food, wheat, corn, and clothes started to grow rapidly. (...) People have money, they sell the cattle with horns on high prices, and other cattle such as pigs and horses. Countrymen sell food and the maximum price of 42 crowns per meter of wheat is not respected. Some people sell it for 200 crowns per meter... The countrymen decide on the maximum price (...) No one set maximum prices for shopkeepers and artisans, so they rip people off (Biber 2003: 282).

What consequences did the First World War have on the way people think about the armed conflicts?

The horrors of war left a deep mark on the participants of the war, the civilians, and the new heir to the throne Karl, who invested his powers, together with his wife Zita to end the war as soon as possible, because they were not ready to tie the Monarchy destiny to German interests, or even worse sacrifice it for its interests.

By summing up impressions from the conversation with their high-positioned guests from Germany[22] both emperor Karl and his minister of external affairs agreed that they do not share the enthusiasm and faith of their allies about the efficiency of the new German military strategy. [...] Emperor Karl invested his energy and hope into prevention of the conflict between Germany and the USA, and thus indirectly save his country (Kardum 2009:206).

---

[22] German state Secretary of Foreign Affairs Arthur Zimmermann and the commander of German Admiralty Hötzendorf informed emperor Karl and Czernin about the new military strategy, i.e. about the German submarine war and the need to use Trieste, Pula and Kotor as submarine bases so that Antanta can not use Mediterranean as the detour for its Atlantic transports.

Care Karlo, nemoj dizat buna,

nije za te ni mađarska kruna.[23]

(Emperor Karl, don't call for revolution,

the Hungarian crown is too much for you anyway)

Trying to find ways to contact the responsible people in the Antanta, without causing suspicion of Germany and Hungary, Emperor Karl decided to use his family connections and contacted the heads of Antanta through empress Zita's brother, Prince Sixtus of Bourbon. From Karl's letter to Sixtus and the note of Its Highness, his empathy towards his subjects and the thriving to end the horrors of war by a separate peace. In Kardum (2009:213) it is quoted: "In hope that this way we would both end the suffering of millions of soldiers and their families who live in anguish and fear, I aks you for a brotherly favour."

Care Karlo pitaj svoje Zite,

smiju li se ženiti komite.[24]

(Emperor Karl, ask Zita

if volunteering soldiers can get married)

Bog poživi tu caricu Zitu,

ona neda ustrelit' komitu.[25]

---

[23] One of the sovereigns was Austrian emperor Karl.

[24] The verses talk about mocking emperor Karl and his permissive nature and submissiveness to his wife's influence.

[25] These verses show the gratitude of Croatian people to emperor's wife Zita and her attitude towards defectors.

(Long live empress Zita,

she won't let volunteering soldiers get shot)

At the beginning the soldiers were *high-spirited,* some of them excited, but most of them got tired of the war duty very soon, because they took part in trench warfare. After the army supply stopped to function, the situation got very difficult among soldiers who had already been weakened by many diseases and war injuries. Soldiers' moral decreased, they were hungry, thirsty, full of fear and disappointment, and due to aimless self-sacrifice they often resorted to self-wounding and the rejection of obedience, i.e. rebellions, surrendering, prison, desertion[26], and truce with enemies[27].

War ailments, death on the battlefield and the like can be seen as a desirable sacrifice for one of the already mentioned higher-purpose values - the ruler, the homeland, honour, nation, family, comrades [...] The everyday of many armed conflicts, actualities of war, do not consist of attacks and counter-attacks, but of suffering from continuing fatigue, sleep deprivation, hunger, commanders, and other 'non-heroic' struggles. Moreover, these struggles can be as deadly as others [...] – for instance being exposed to long-range shelling or infectious diseases (Hameršak 2013: 391).

Zbogom, zbogom, moja diko mila,

sutra će me oterat Rusija.[28]

---

[26] More about the appearance of volunteering army (komita) or Green staff in Slavonia and a different vision of their existence in Georg von Trapp, *To the Last Salute XIII*, Zagreb, 1917., Slavko Janković, *Šokačke pismice*, part 2, Vinkovci, 1970, *Kronika Franjevačkog samostana u Brodu na Savi IV (1879-1932)*, edited by P. Egidija Stjepana Bibera, Slavonski Brod, 2003.

[27] More on phenomenon of spontaneous peace treaties around Christmas and Eastern in Hameršak, F., *Tamna strana Marsa*, 238.

[28] One of the rare verses which is sung by a soldier who wants to be captured in Russian attack.

(Goodbye, goodbye, my darling,
tommorow I will be chased away by Russia)

U Rusiji baš na kolodvoru,
tamo su mi zarobili lolu.

(In Russia, at the station,
that's where my darling was arrested)

Jao moje nadaleko roblje,
s tobom mlada leći ću u groblje.

(Oh, my slave far away,
I will lie in the grave with you, so young)

How did the subject of the First World War coexist in the everyday life of conflict and tolerance?

It was a duty of all men to go to the war. Women, similarly to soldiers, dealt with it differently. They sang proudly about their pain and suffering, and there are many verses of *bećarac* that speak of that. Those verses talk about their feelings:

Oj soldatu, kako je u ratu?
Bome gorko bez tebe, divojko!

(Hey, soldier, what's the war like?
Well, it's rough without you, girl)

Da j' mi doći u vojničku četu,

pružit ruku mojemu janjetu.

(If I could come to military unit,

to give my darling a hand)

Dika mi je kod kraljeve garde,

Cara služi, a meni se tuži.[29]

(My darling is in the royal service,

he serves the emperor and complains to me)

empathy:

Neću nosit ni srme ni zlata,

dok mi dika ne dojde iz rata.

(I will not wear embroidery nor gold,

until my darling comes from the war)

Oj kako ću ja vesela biti,

a moj dragi kod cara giniti!

(Oh, how can I be happy,

when my darling is going to die for the emperor)

---

[29] Soldier is complaining about the non-human army conditions.

Piše dika, da je u špitalju.
Jadan kuka, ranita mu ruka.

(My darling writes to me from the hosiptal;
poor him, he cries that his arm has been wounded)

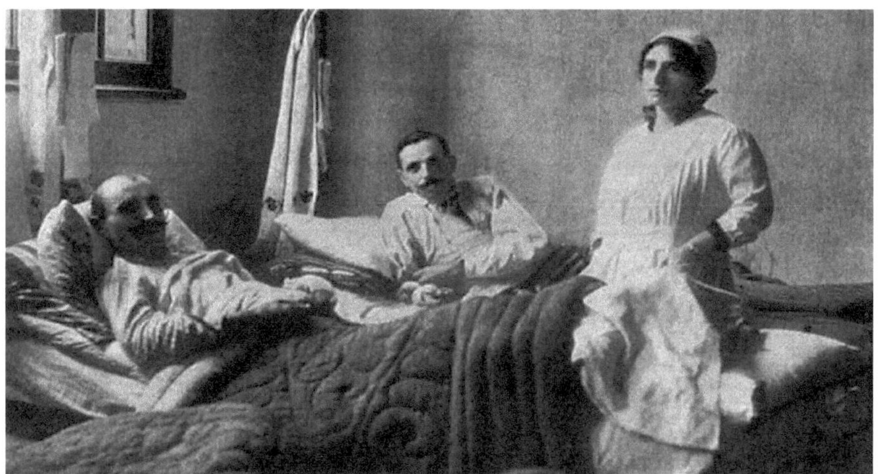

Picture 7. Wounded soldiers

anticipation:

Da Bog dade, da se rat umiri,
da se cveće do mene došeće.

(If only God would make the war calm down,
so my darling would walk towards me)

Piši diko na biloj artiji,
kako ti je u marškumpaniji.

(My darling, write to me on a white piece of paper,
tell me how you are doing in the war)

Meni dika iz Rusije piše:
Janje moje, mene zarobiše.

(My darling writes to me from Russia:
Dear, I have been captured)

Picture 8. Correspondence from the First World War

anxiety:

Mili Bože, i ovoga rata,
oće l' dika dojti iz soldata.

(Dear God, this war;
will my darling return from the army?)

Ruski care, Boga ne vidio,
što si moje zlato zarobio!

(Russian emperor, be cursed
for capturing my darling)

Piši, diko, meni sa jabane,
nek mi mladoj na srcu odlane.

(Write to me, my darling, from the faraway land,
make my young heart feel better)

fears:

Oj komito, ja bi te klela,
Da ja nemam komitu dilbera.

(Oh, volunteering army, I would curse you
if my darling wasn't a volunteering soldier)

Stra' me rata, ostat ću bez zlata
Ako pade, ja mlada ostade.

(I am afraid of war, I will lose my darling;
If he falls, I will stay alone young)

Saletila vrana sa jablana,
Dobila sam pismo od dragana.[30]

(The crow flew from far away,
I got a letter from my darling)

restlessness:

Caruj care, al' nemoj zbog rata,
jer zbog rata osta neudata.

(Rule, you emperor, but not becuase of war;
for the war has left me unmarried)

Drage druge, sad nije sramota,
ovog rata biti (ostat) neudata.

(Dear girlfriends, it is not a shame
to be (stay) unmarried in this war)

Mili Bože, al' se bitka bije,
nema 'noga, tko zaplako nije.

---

[30] The girl received bad news from the battlefield, because crow is a symbol of bad news, or death.

Picture 9. Consequences of the First World War

There were attempts to excite national pride of soldiers by different propaganda and press releases to defend their country and hate the enemy. But as the war progressed, enthusiasm faded, and the demonization of the opponent was completely or partly extinguished. As Filip Hameršak (2013:572) says "this was not about some abstract humanism, but a version of the *golden rule* 'do not treat others as you would not like to be treated yourself', based on some sort of common interest, or quid pro quo idea - you have to help others, because one day they will help you."

In the times of occupation of certain territories, there are records of good relationships between the occupying army and the occupied population:

(Italian woman, take care of my darling,

make him coffee, take care of my darling)

Serbian women made sure to keep our soldiers warm, because they must have had their husbands in mind, who defended their homeland bravely and painstakingly. On many occasions did some of the ladies cook food for tired soldiers... (Knežević 2004:128). Women across Soča were beautiful, thin, elastic and lovely. If they were hot-blooded and good towards others, that would be one crazy fairy-tale. They were hungry, as well as their children, so they kept their honour (Blašković 2014:50).

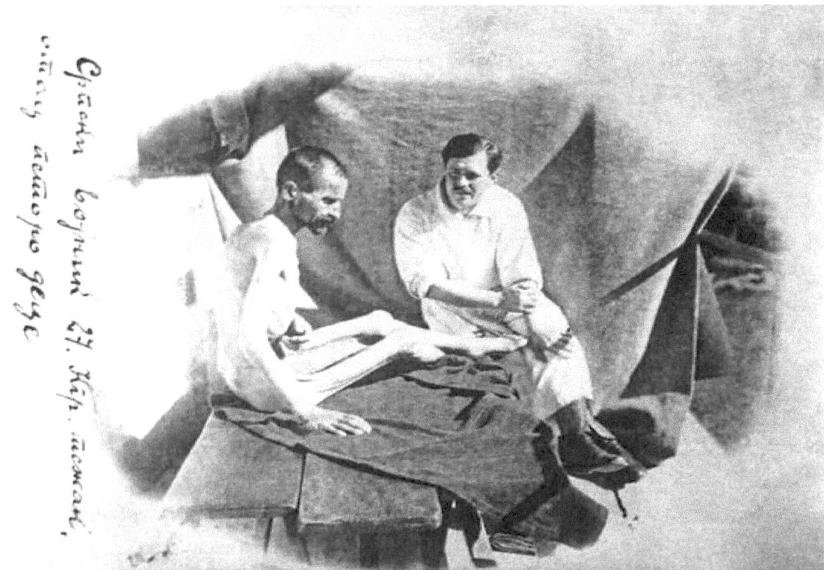

Picture 10. The appearance of soldiers after the First World War[31]

---

[31] The consequences of the War were catastrophic. For example after the War some soldiers weighed only 27 kg (59 lb 8.397 oz)

How reliable is the representation of the First World War in the verses?

Bećarac belongs to the oral literature. Its main feature is its minimalistic form which is apparent both in the expression and content. Its lyricism is visible in the focus on emotions and inner experience of the subject who uses verse to express different feelings and to give realistic information about experience, life, relationships, and historical events, too. This is confirmed by Užarević (2010:114): "It contains elements of historical events and life circumstances – starting from the times of the Military Frontier and the occupation of Bosnia across the tragic battlefields of the First World War (Serbia, Galicia, Russia) to the dissolution of Austro-Hungarian Monarchy and farther."

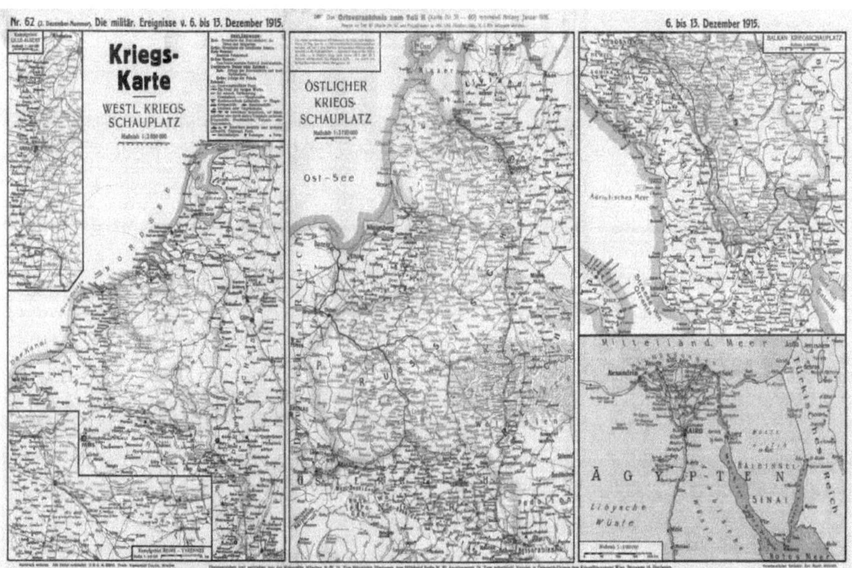

Picture 11. Map of the Western, Eastern, Balkan and Russian-Turkish battlefields

Crn se oblak priko neba vije,
moj se dragi s Talijanom bije.

(Black cloud is hanging in the sky,
my darling is fighting against Italians)

Crn se oblak priko neba vuče,
sad se dika Albanijom tuče.

(Black sky is drifting across the sky,
now my darling is fighting against Albania)

Diko moja, kad dojdeš do Drine,
'itaj zgode, pa mi piši, rode.

(My darling, when you come to Drina,
write to me)

Galicijo, sva krvi zalita,
tamo mi je dika baš ranita.

(Galicia, all in blood,
there my darling was wounded)

Italijo, pokrilo te cveće,
kud se moje janje često šeće.

(Italy, covered in flowers,
there my darling walks a lot)

Po Srbiji povenilo cveće,
mene dika više vidit neće.

(In Serbia the flowers have withered,
my darling won't see me anymore)

Oj Rusijo, alaj si daleko,
mila diko, ko bi te doviko.

(Oh, Russia, you are so far away;
my darling, who will call your name)

Trojica mi iz Srbije pišu,
da je dika zarobit u Nišu.

(Three men are writing from Serbia
that my darling has been captured in Niš)

Kud se moje obasulo grožđe,
po Karpati, žalosna mu mati.

(Where my grapes have fallen?
All over Karpati, poor him)

So, in the quoted verses there are lots of information on historical events of the First World War. For example, besides the battle location[32] (Russia, Albany, Italy, Galicia), we find out about the battlefield scenery, terrors of being wounded, dying, forms of battles, i.e. war techniques (trench warfare, capturing enemies), war machinery and artillery (bombs, machine guns, guns, bayonets, grenades, heavy artillery), treating patients in army hospitals, (bad) weather conditions (high water level), communication of family members or engaged couples (although correspondence was censored, and writing and sending letters was almost impossible during cross fire, and there are not much available data on that). Hameršak (2013:610) says: "Correspondence of families, the engaged couples, and similar is rarely mentioned [...] mostly in connection to the complications with its delivery. [...] since the correspondence was under censorship and it needed to be thematically adapted."

---

[32] In the regiments in Slavonia, soldiers from Brod and the surroundings fought in the south battlefield in Serbia (battles at Cer and Kolubara) and in Russia with occasional success, and in Galicia, Bukovina, Bessarabia and southwest battlefield of Italy with great human losses (battles near Piava and at the river Soca); in Cafuta, I., *Iza bojišnice – živjeti u Brodu na Savi 1914. – 1918.*, 16.

Picture 12. Battlefiled with corpses

Bila bluza i zelena gomba[33]
moga diku ranila je bomba.

(White shirt and green pendant,
my darling was wounded by a bomb)

Diku mi je pogodilo tane,
u zlo misto u obrve vrane.

(My darling was hit by a bullet,
in a bad spot, into his dark eyebrows)

---

[33] Round decorative pendant.

Picture 13. The powerful German howitzer M-Gerät known in history as Fat Bertha

Italijo, krvlju zalivena,
tamo mi je dika ubijena.

(Italy, covered in blood,
 that's where my darling was killed)

Kolega mi dvi karte poslao,
da je dika u Rusiji pao.

(My colleague sent me two cards,
saying that my darling fell down in Russia)

Mila mamo, ranjeno mi dere,

ranjeno je iz mašingevere.

(Dear mother, my darling was shot,
shot from the machine gun)

U Rusiji i blato i suša,
tamo mi je i srce i duša.

(In Russia there is both mud and drought,
my heart and soul are there, too)

Picture 14. Trench warfare

Na ratištu padaje granate…
Pazi, diko, da ne padnu na te.

(The grenades are flying over the battlefield,
be careful, darling, not to get hit)

Oj Rusijo, u tebi topovi,
ginu momci kano golubovi.

(Hey, Russia, in you there are cannons,
young boys get killed like pigeons)

U Rusiji voda do koljena,
tamo mi je želja zarobljena.

(In Russia water is at knee level,
my wish is captured there)

Rascvala se gorušica žuta,
u dekungu kraj mlada regruta.

(Yellow mustard is in blossom,
in the trench next to the young soldier)

Sava nosi drvlje i kamenje,
a Morava dragana krvava.

(The Sava carries wood and stones,
and the Morava my darling in blood)

Srce moje Galiciji teži,
di moj dragi u dekungu leži.

(My heart goes to Galicia,
where my darling lies in the trench)

Picture 15. Detail from the battlefiled

Na Rusiji jedno brdo malo,
tamo j' moje janje zakopano.

(There is a small hill in Russia
where my darling has been buried)

These numerous verses are a proof that the war is a greedy monster, an ill beast, an unjustifiable act of wounding, killing and destruction, a dangerous form of expressing dissatisfaction, and an immoral act of reaching some goals.

Picture 16. An exhausted soldier in a trench

Conclusion

Since the analysed form is a minimal poetic structure and it belongs to the literary-artistic genre, which makes it lyric and subjective, it is difficult to fight the impression that content in *bećarac* is historically authentic and very objective.

No literary text should be taken as a direct insight, of course; we need to be aware of its selective, intentional or unintentional perspectivity and therefore stay sceptic methodically and if possible compare it to what other texts say (both literary and historical or legal ones), taking into consideration so called helping historical sciences (Žmegač 1982:81).

But the very detailed analysis of some other texts, listed in the references, such as historical monographs, chronicles and catalogues, and autobiographical sources of war participants, show that this poetic form is a good source, a mirror or a window to the world of the First World War events. It can tell a lot about horrors of the war, battle locations, relationship between the comrades, economic or political situation in the countries, political sovereigns, and at the same time we can focus on the emotion and the inner experiences of the direct war participants, as well as the one who waited for them at home (slightly less, we must admit).

Picture 17. Women in the First World War

These verses are not sung by women who listened about the war, but the ones who lived these horrors. Therefore, to understand and explain the content of *bećarac* with the topic of war, this is a very important piece of information.

Those we love never truly leave us.
There are things that death cannot touch.

Jack Thorne

Sources

1. Janković, S. (1967) *Šokačke pismice, part 1*. Vinkovci: Matica hrvatska.

2. Janković, S. (1970): *Šokačke pismice, part 2*. Vinkovci: Matica hrvatska.

3. Lukić, L. *Crtice ili zapiske iz rata 1915.-1918.*, E/T/19, 33, Muzej Brodskoga Posavlja Manuscript collection of Luka Lukić in the Museum of Brodsko Posavlje.

4. Lukić, L. *Oprisavačke priskočnice*, Manuscript collection of Luka Lukić in the Museum of Brodsko Posavlje.

5. Lukić, L. *Kaniške priskočnice*, Manuscript collection of Luka Lukić in the Museum of Brodsko Posavlje.

6. Lukić, L. *Varoške pjesme*, Manuscript collection of Luka Lukić in the Museum of Brodsko Posavlje.

7. Lukić, L. *Priskočnice što se govore u kolu, kraće pjesme iz Varoša*, Manuscript collection of Luka Lukić in the Museum of Brodsko Posavlje.

8. Lukić, L. *Stare pjesme iz Varoša*, Manuscript collection of Luka Lukić in the Museum of Brodsko Posavlje.

9. Copy of the Brlić family archive, box 74, bundle 7, recording DD00103101.

References

1. Biber, P. E. S. (Ed). (2003) Kronika Franjevačkog samostana u Brodu na Savi IV (1879-1932). Slavonski Brod: Matica hrvatska Ogranak Slavonski Brod.

2. Blašković, P. (2014) *Sa Bošnjacima u svjetskom ratu*. Strmec Samoborski: Fortuna.

3. Cafuta I. (2014): *Iza bojišnice - živjeti u Brodu na Savi 1914.-1918.* Slavonski Brod: Muzej Brodskog Posavlja.

4. Goldstein, I. (2008) *Hrvatska povijest*, knj.21. Zagreb. Biblioteka Jutarnjeg lista.

5. Hameršak, F. (2013) *Tamna strana Marsa*. Zagreb: Naklada Ljevak.

6. Hutinec, G. Ed. (2008). *Prvi svjetski rat i poslijeratna Europa (1914.-1936.),* book 16, (translation Ana Badurina). Zagreb. Biblioteka Jutarnjega lista.

7. Kardum, L. (2009): *Suton stare Europe*, Zagreb, Golden marketing – Tehnička knjiga.

8 Knežević, B. (2014). *Gledanje u vidjeno: ratovanje u Srbiji 1914. Godine.* Strmec Samoborski: Fortuna.

9. Krile, D. (2014) Prešućena povijest, Zašto je zaborav pokrio sve hrvatske žrtve Prvoga svjetskog rata. Available at:

http://www.slobodnadalmacija.hr/Hrvatska/tabid/66/articleType/ArticleView/articlel d/242698/Default.aspx. (Retrieved on March 9, 2015).

10. MacMillan, M. (2008) *Mirotovorci*. Zagreb: Naklada Ljevak.

11. Užarević, J. (2009) Poetika bećarca, *Šokačka rič 7*, (Ed. Anica Bilić), Vinkovci, Zajednica kulturno-umjetničkih djelatnosti Vukovarsko-srijemske županije u Vinkovcima, 111-139.

12. Smetko, A. Ed. (2011) *Dadoh zlato za željezo - Hrvatska u Prvom svjetskom ratu 1914.-1918.* Zagreb: Hrvatski povijesni muzej.

13. Von Trapp, G. (1917) *To the Last Salute XII.* Zagreb.

14. Žmegač, V. (1982): *Književnost i zbilja.* Zagreb: Školska knjiga.

*Note – All images are downloaded from the Internet.

Printed by Books on Demand GmbH, Norderstedt / Germany